HOPE

FOR MOMS

HOPE
FOR MOMS

IT'S TOUGH OUT THERE, BUT SO ARE YOU

ANNA MCARTHUR

BEAVER'S POND
PRESS

Edited by Angela Wiechmann
Cover artwork by Yawen Chien
Cover and book design by Abbie Phelps
Heart divider image © Adobe Stock / koltukovs

Text is set in Adobe Caslon Pro

ISBN 13: 978-1-64343-560-2
Library of Congress Catalog Number: 2024924671
Printed in the United States
First Edition 2025
29 28 27 26 25   5 4 3 2 1

BEAVER'S POND PRESS

Beaver's Pond Press
939 West Seventh Street
Saint Paul, MN 55102
(952) 829-8818
www.BeaversPondPress.com

To order, visit www.itascabooks.com
Contact the author at www.annamcarthur.com for speaking engagements and interviews.

In memory of my grandmother Frances Hinton Sledd Olson, who always reminded me that "This too shall pass." I now know that it was both a promise and a warning; the passing is bittersweet.

Contents

NO: THESE THINGS GO

MAYBE: WE'LL DO OUR BEST GOING FORWARD

Prologue

HI THERE, LOVE. It's tough, isn't it?

One truth of parenthood is that you never quite feel qualified for such an important job. As soon as you figure out a phase one of your kids is going through or a challenge they're facing, they move on to something new. And what you learn from one kid doesn't necessarily help with the next one. It can feel like a game of Whac-A-Mole, and it can be really isolating.

As a parent of four children, I often look around and wonder, "Does everyone else know what they're doing? Is this only hard for me? How do other families look so put-together, yet we can't ever find our shoes?"

When my oldest daughter, Caroline, was diagnosed with dyslexia . . . when my son, Caleb, came out as gay at a rural high school in Georgia . . . when my adopted African American twins, Elizabeth and

KD, asked hard questions about their skin color . . . whenever we've faced a storm as a family . . . I've wondered if we were doing something wrong. I've felt cast out to sea. It's been awful.

I've been a mom for over twenty years, and I can tell you this much is true: Every mom is thrown curveballs. I've been thrown more than I ever could have imagined.

When we decided to adopt—after having two biological children, who were then in kindergarten and first grade—I wasn't prepared for how much our family would change. Some of it was due to the super-fast adoption process. And some of it was due to not yet knowing the challenges that would arise from caring for premie twins. I also wasn't prepared for the fact that raising kids of a different race would make our family different. I didn't know how *interesting* we'd be as a whole.

Caroline and Caleb are now out of college, and Elizabeth and KD are in high school. I wouldn't change anything about our four awesome kids. But I've had to learn how to be a different kind of mom for each one of them. Sometimes, many times over.

Being a mom is so hard. It can feel kind of

impossible. It can feel like you're making it up as you go.

But you're doing your best. And you aren't alone. You can't stop hard things from coming your way, but you can learn from your experiences and decide which lessons are worth keeping.

A few years ago, my husband, Bryan, crashed during a mountain bike race and had to have major knee surgery. He couldn't drive for six weeks. The twins were starting kindergarten, and the older kids were in middle school. It was overwhelming to figure out four kids' schedules plus Bryan's rehab with me as the only driver.

We needed triage.

In a moment of determined reasonableness, I went right to the large black Pottery Barn chalkboard we kept in one corner of our kitchen. It was the place where I wrote out all the kids' activities and our various appointments so that everyone in the family could see them. (Bryan would sometimes take a picture of it. That way, he didn't have to ask me a thousand times which day was soccer.)

On this chalkboard, I sketched out a triage of sorts, dividing the activities into three categories:

YES: These things were "absolutely necessary" at that stage in our life. This included school, Bryan's physical therapy, Elizabeth's vision therapy, and keeping Bryan's business operating (not only for the sake of our family but also for the twenty employees who depended on it).

NO: These things "weren't going to happen." This included optional activities, like birthday parties, school fundraisers, and big gatherings where no one was expecting us.

MAYBE: These things "would be good." This included a reasonable amount of sleep for us all, exercise for me, and the kids' sports and activities we'd already committed to.

The triage system helped us survive those six weeks. It kept us focused on what was truly important to us.

Once Bryan was well, we no longer needed triage, so I reverted the chalkboard back to our usual list of activities and appointments. Nevertheless, I kept the system in my mind. After six weeks of viewing life through a Yes, No, and Maybe lens, I realized that so many *mandatory* things—not just activities and invitations but mindsets and beliefs—were actually optional.

Very, very optional.

I've written this book as a sort of triage for moms in the thick of it. Using the same Yes, No, and Maybe categories from our chalkboard, I share stories, experiences, and lessons I've learned as a mom.

I want you to feel empowered to decide which lessons from motherhood you want to keep, which bits and pieces you want to let go of, and which areas you want to nurture going forward. At the end of each chapter, I've listed some questions or prompts to help you reflect on your own experiences and hopes.

I wish that each child came with a step-by-step guide, but that hasn't been my experience. Growth isn't linear—for kids or moms. Over the years, I've had to circle the same lesson a few times before I've finally gotten it. As you read, you'll find that some themes, stories, and lessons circle as well, showing up in different sections.

One of my favorite Indigo Girls lyrics says, "You'll never fly as the crow flies. Get used to the country mile." I'm very grateful that you're coming along on this journey with me.

YES

THESE THINGS STAY

CHAPTER 1

Remember to keep accepting help.

WE WERE DEFINITELY causing a scene. My two-year-old daughter, Caroline, had decided that she didn't want to leave preschool. She didn't want to go home, so she was going big. She sat down in the parking lot, stopping traffic with her one-girl sit-in.

My infant son, Caleb, was crying in his carrier. I held the carrier in the crook of one arm and tried to scoop my daughter off the pavement with my other hand. The diaper bag over my shoulder kept swinging into my son's face.

A mom I'd never met walked over. She was slightly older than me. "Can I help you with one of them?" she asked.

"No, thanks," I said. "I've got it."

"I don't think you do," she said.

Without missing a beat, she asked which car was mine, took the carrier off my arm, and walked Caleb to the car so I was free to wrestle my toddler off the ground.

Why did I say "No, thanks"? I clearly didn't *have* it, like I claimed. Why didn't I just accept the help she was offering?

Why didn't I even recognize her actions as an offer of help? In my head, all I heard was judgment: *Why is this so hard for you? No one else's kids are hugging the pavement and backing up traffic. You better get those kids under control now, or you are going to have wild kids on your hands for the rest of your life.*

Part of it was that I was a new mom. I was pretty insecure and overwhelmed and lonely. I thought I was the only mom who was struggling. I was so eager to get it right that I couldn't admit any vulnerability, even when I desperately needed help.

I think about this mom often. She taught me how to accept help. And to offer it.

None of us are really prepared to raise our kids. I can't count the number of times I've said to my husband, "I should have majored in something else—something that could actually help me." Nursing. Early childhood education. Psychology. Cattle wrangling.

Instead, I majored in sociology and women's studies in college and then earned a master of divinity in seminary. None of these things prepared me for being a mom. In some ways, women's studies hurt me—I felt like I was letting the whole sisterhood down by staying home with my kids.

What my education did do, however, was build the foundational truth that none of us are in this alone. "We're all in this together," as *High School Musical* reminds us.

I've finally figured out that we regularly need help. Saying we *don't* is just a waste of time and energy. It's also a missed opportunity to connect to other families. Good things happen when I walk into a room and say "I need help" or "What am I missing?"

I still mess up with my kids all the time.

Full disclosure: I accidentally left sixth-grade

Caleb at home when I headed out to teach a Sunday school class on *parenting*. I didn't even realize it until after the class, when I saw a text from him that said "Forget something?" I'd walked right past him sitting on the couch, jumped in my car, then blabbed on for an hour about "intentional parenting." [Insert facepalm emoji.]

But I don't let these mess-ups knock the wind out of me like I used to. I do the best I can with what information I have. And when I don't know what to do, I get quiet and start paying attention to the people around me. Who has been brought into my life that could be a gift during this season?

Then I tell fear that she isn't the boss of me and that she needs to pipe down.

Sure, there are moms who have their act together more than I do. There are kids who are easier than mine. There are families that don't cause scenes. But that's not who we are.

I have to believe that this family of mine was chosen for one another; that we didn't randomly find one another. This family of six is who we were meant to be. When I can stand in that truth, I don't doubt myself or my parenting abilities too much.

Is there a mom you know that you can encourage or help?

Can you think of a time when you accepted help? How did that change things?

CHAPTER 2

Remember that it's okay to cry about your situation.

THIS IS A hill I will die on: Grief is a part of motherhood.

As someone who struggled with postpartum depression, I understood—even in the midst of it—that I was grieving something. Or someone. I was so unexpectedly and profoundly changed when I became a mom. There was a before and an after, and I was in the after.

It was good stuff: I had a healthy baby girl, a super-involved husband, and friends who celebrated our daughter's birth with us. But it was also brutal stuff: She had colic and cried every night for hours, I was leaking milk at work and pumping between church services, and everything had changed.

I grieved, and then I adjusted. Because that's what we have to do to keep our households and our lives running.

My second child was born just fifteen months later, ushering in a new wave of exhaustion and worry. By that time, no one doubted I needed medication.

We'd spent so much time prepping for labor and delivery, but then they just sent us home with these vulnerable and loud little creatures. I definitely wasn't properly trained for parenthood. Some days, just keeping them alive was the absolute best I could do. There were plenty of days when leaving the house required the logistics and precision of a military operation.

Here's what I know now that I wish I'd known then: It's okay to say out loud, to someone trustworthy, "This isn't what I thought I was signing up for. I don't know if I can do this. I'm kind of a flight risk. Can you come over?"

Being a mom is super hard—not because you're doing anything wrong, but just because it is.

Being a mom is super hard by default, so if you add in complications—like disabilities or adoption or family trauma—then there will be some tears. And that's perfectly normal.

"Would anyone *enjoy* what you're doing?" a therapist once said, when I'd explained the details of my daily life with four kids.

I laughed because it was kind of rude. But later, I found it validating. She—a young single woman—was essentially saying, "I wouldn't want your life right now. It sounds awful!"

It helped me realize that I wasn't doing a rotten job of managing my life—I was just on a harder path than most. It gave me some moxie.

It also cleared some space for me to see the ways my kids were struggling.

I can't speak for all adoptions, but most of the ones I've seen firsthand have some undergirding of trauma and grief. Something has gone "wrong," individually or systemically, in order for an adoption to be necessary. A support system has disappeared.

Systemic racism has created generational poverty. Moms have been left on their own, or dads have been disenfranchised.

That grief, that ache, doesn't go away for the adoptee just because they are adopted. I've seen my twins struggle with a kind of homesickness for a place or family they can't name.

I've been changed by adoption as well. In the great Broadway musical *Wicked*, one of the characters sings, "Something has changed within me; something is not the same." I feel this way about being an adoptive mom—especially in regard to race. I can't go back to who I was before or unlearn what I now know.

There's liturgy that's often used in worship that states, "Your old life has gone and a new one has begun." It's meant to be an acknowledgment of a cleansing, a promise of fresh starts.

But it also means your old life is *gone*. It's okay to grieve that old life; it doesn't mean the new one won't be wonderful.

Make a list of people you can call or text when motherhood gets too heavy.

Is there something you need to grieve? Give yourself permission to face it head on, handle it, and come out stronger on the other side . . . even if it takes a while.

CHAPTER 3

Remember that you can't protect your kids from heartache.

I SUPPOSE A mom can never know how she'll respond to seeing her kids struggle or get hurt. But me—I've been surprised by how many times I've wanted to burn down buildings. It's like a flare that comes out of nowhere when someone intentionally hurts one of my kids.

I recently felt this way about our local school. Another student told sweet Elizabeth, who has beautiful dark skin, that her skin looked like "charcoal." She was devastated, and I clearly overreacted. It wasn't the whole school's fault; I just wanted to protect her.

But I'm learning over and over again that I can't protect my kids from cruelty or heartache or disappointment.

I can only make sure they know that I'm always in their corner.

Most humans can withstand unbelievable difficulties—*if* they know they aren't alone.

I remember the day in seminary when a professor literally stood at the side of the pulpit as three different students came forward to share hard truths. The professor's physical presence was noteworthy to me. It's one thing to tell people you have their back; it's another to show them that in real life.

I've seen this in people accompanying their sibling to divorce court. In friends doing housecleaning for someone in chemotherapy. In young moms sitting with one another through postpartum depressions. In thousands of small ways that demonstrate that love means showing up.

One of the best things we can say to one another is "Would you like me to come with you?"

Even if the other people decline, they'll remember the offer.

They'll remember who showed up.

At some point, most parents will be in over their heads.

When we adopted KD and Elizabeth, I naively thought we were ready to handle premie twins of a race different from our own. In reality, I hadn't done enough work and reflection. I'd confused being progressive with being antiracist.

If the twins had been raised in a Black family, I think they would have been forewarned about some of the intolerance they would inevitably face. But all I basically did was hold my breath, hoping people would be kind. It was magical thinking.

It didn't last very long.

As a preschooler, KD told us she didn't like her brown skin and asked when her skin would turn white like ours. That same year, a little boy told Elizabeth that their preschool slide wasn't for people with brown skin. I was unprepared for all this and thus hadn't prepared them for it.

I'm more realistic now. I walk into a room

differently. I scan spaces for people of color. I notice who holds the microphone at events and whose time is cut short. I seek out families that look like ours.

Sure, all of this awareness is well and good. It's a new lens through which I view the world, and I'm thankful. But I need to acknowledge that I didn't have this lens *until* I became an adoptive mom. And my new awareness is powerless to stop the racism and prejudice that floods my twins' lives.

I'm more protective of them and their precious hearts as they've grown older. I'm actually fiercely protective of all four of my kids. I've gotten pretty good at looking for clues that tell me if our family will be welcomed or not. As a family, we're *too interesting* for some places and people.

It's okay because we know we're awesome, as individuals and as a family. If places aren't welcoming, I've learned that we can just walk away.

We don't have to burn anything down on our way out.

The writer Glennon Doyle has said, "We grown-ass people do what we need to do to follow our truth. We don't have to be defensive—we can afford to be gentle because we know what's right for us. Those who disapprove will either come around or stop coming around. Either way, lovely."

Lovely, indeed.

What phrases do you find reassuring? What do you want your kids to remember you saying to them regularly?

Has anyone stood beside you or shown you that they have your back? How did it make you feel?

CHAPTER 4

Remember that running on empty isn't a badge of honor.

To KICK OFF a retreat workshop I lead called "Soul Care for Moms," I set out a bunch of magazines and ask the moms to make a collage of things that bring them joy. Not things that *should* make them happy, but rather things that actually make their hearts jump. I remind them that they aren't trying to impress anyone; if they enjoy reality television, they shouldn't cut out images of triathlon training.

This activity can be jarring. As moms, we can tell you exactly what our family's preferences are, but we often literally forget what we ourselves like. In particular, I've noticed a pattern with moms who have kids younger than age ten: This activity makes them cry. No one has asked them about *their* joy lately. They truly don't know.

I feel strongly about this: As moms, we shouldn't go years without considering our own wants and desires.

There's a lot of talk in "mom world" about self-care, and that's awesome. But I'm not talking about spa days or bubble baths. Those are nice things, but they won't fix not being seen or attended to or cherished.

True self-care is much harder to fit into our lives. It requires that we respect ourselves and teach others to respect us. It means being truthful about what is nourishing us and what is sucking us dry. It expects us to speak up and sometimes make a scene so that we don't disappear.

I have an amazing husband, but if I keep putting myself at the bottom of the list every single time, he can't fix that. I also have very caring parents, but it's not their job to know what I need. I am the boss of making sure I am okay.

This is especially true when something happens

with my family that really stings. When Caleb left for college, a dear friend said to me, "This is not the time for Holocaust movies. This is ice cream time." In tough times, we moms are allowed to cut back and take a minute to regroup.

Unfortunately, self-care is sometimes pitched to us as a transactional kind of practice. We are instructed to fill up our tanks, only so we can care for others. I get this. I know I need to take care of myself so I'm strong enough to help my family weather crises.

But I also need to take care of myself simply because I deserve to be cared for as a human being. *What if we filled up our tanks because we are worthy of that kind of love?*

I remember seeing a poster that said, "A mom is only as happy as her unhappiest child." I wanted to throw something. I have four kids—that's quite a game of hot potato if I have to make sure they're all okay before I can be okay.

Here's one thing I've figured out: We are allowed to have peace and joy even when our kids are struggling. It doesn't mean we don't see their hurt or feel their pain viscerally; it means we don't have to be pulled underwater by it.

Every once in a while, I think, *I might have this parenting thing basically under control. I haven't left a child at school or dropped them off at the wrong activity in a while. The kids and animals are all vaccinated. It's been a few weeks since we had SpongeBob mac and cheese for dinner. Things are going so well that I might even learn how to make bread or figure out how to can some vegetables or finally solve those termite problems we have in our house.*

It's a glorious feeling of competency. My mom calls it "having your bat." She might have made it up, but it basically means that even though baseballs are flying at you, you have your bat, and you're able to knock each of those balls out of the park.

There are other days, though, when the balls keep coming but I can't find my bat anywhere. I shouldn't just stand there, getting clobbered. But sometimes I do.

Another way to think about it is to imagine your car's gas light coming on, yet you just keep driving. That's what I do sometimes as a mom.

I've learned the hard way that ignoring the gas light on my car isn't a great solution. Why do I think ignoring the "gauge" of my own body and spirit will be any different?

I hit a rough patch a few years ago that woke me up to the downside of running on fumes.

It wasn't depression—I know what depression feels like. For me, it feels like waking up wearing a heavy suit of armor and knowing you still have to go about your regular day.

This was different. I felt numb.

I think the adrenaline of adopting the twins had just worn off. I was in the middle of a child-rearing marathon, but I'd been running it like a sprint. And it had left me feeling a little vacant. That emptiness was pretty scary.

No one benefits from a mom who thinks she can somehow just keep going when she's running on fumes. So now when I feel my gas tank rapidly depleting, I know that I just need a little time by myself.

I'm an introvert who lives with four, sometimes five, tornadoes. My husband and all three daughters have energy spilling out of them. It's a loud and lively house.

Sometimes, I just need to leave town to remember that I exist beyond my own household and that there's a whole big world out there. I need to be still and quiet. Then, I'll be ready for the next thing and the thing after that.

When I'm at my strongest, I know that I'm hearty enough for this life that we've built. When I'm not at my strongest, yet my family still needs me, I remember this brilliant quote from author Reynolds Price: "Strength just comes in one brand—you stand up at sunrise and meet what they send you and keep your hair combed."

Tomorrow, I'll wake up and comb my hair. I'll find my bat. I'll be ready.

Make a list of what you truly enjoy.

How do you fill your gas tank?

CHAPTER 5

Remember that raising a family is really hard for everyone.

EVEN IN THE easiest of circumstances, there will be areas where we as parents drop the ball when it comes to raising our children. It's simply not possible to anticipate everything they might need. And if there are extenuating circumstances in your family, such as adoption, there will be an extra-steep learning curve.

Several years ago, right before Christmas, Bryan

was reading to KD from our illustrated children's Bible.

"Why do angels always have blonde hair?" KD asked.

"Not all angels have blonde hair . . ." he responded while flipping through the pages, looking for any non-blonde angels. He kept flipping and flipping.

This was just a regular, mainline Protestant children's Bible. Not a special Bible for only people of European descent. But all the angels were blonde.

Our twins are not blonde, of course. They are gorgeous African American girls who we adopted into our very white family.

This line of questioning made Bryan very nervous, so he called me into the twins' room for some theological backup. I reminded her that Jesus had brown skin, and I said that it was probably just that one Bible.

As soon as I left her bedroom, I started looking through our other Bibles and our Christmas books. I could find only blonde angels, mostly with blue eyes.

Rest assured, I have nothing against blondes. Caleb was blond as a child. I was blonde until middle school. Some of my best friends are blondes. I am not a blondist.

I do find it odd, though, that blondes have somehow managed to take over the angel-marketing department. Were there even blondes yet when Jesus was born in Bethlehem? When were blondes invented? I don't know. I'm not an archaeologist. Maybe they existed up in Scandinavia at the time, but I'm pretty sure most Middle Easterners didn't look like Taylor Swift back then—and don't look like her now.

I imagined how it would feel to be a seven-year-old girl with mahogany-brown skin and dark hair who couldn't see any angels, anywhere, who looked anything like her. Why didn't God's messengers ever look like her? I felt awful that KD felt left out. And I felt even worse that I'd never noticed all the blonde angels until she pointed it out.

I woke up at four o'clock the next morning, convinced that my twins would grow up to not love Jesus because I'd inadvertently brought Aryan angels into our home. Our house was filled with books about adoption, loving our hair, and diverse families. I'd practically memorized their favorite books: *I Like Myself*, *The Skin You Live In*, and *Black*

Is Brown Is Tan. I was horrified that our Christian books were the ones giving us trouble.

During that early-morning panic, I remembered some folk art angel paintings I'd seen posted online by a local artist named Jackie. They were simple and beautiful, but most of those angels were blonde too.

I knew I needed to get in touch with Jackie. I waited until dawn—and until some of the crazy wore off. (I've heard that some people think boundaries are important.) Then I took a chance and sent her a message that said something like, "I have an unusual request. I've seen your angel paintings and think they are gorgeous. Would you be open to making some for our family but with brown skin? I need them to be angels of color."

She was generous and open-hearted and got to work.

I originally thought I would put these paintings where the twins would see them every day, like over their beds or in the playroom. But when I brought these angels into our house, I knew they needed a broader audience. The white people in our family needed these images burned into our brains just as much as the twins did.

These two angels are similar in skin tone and hair

and shape, but they are also distinct. Just like my girls. The angels are featureless and timeless and stunning.

The angel paintings hang on either side of our kitchen table. It's the place where we gather most as a family. These angels of color are watching over us as we eat meals, work on homework, and talk about our days.

One of Caleb's friends walked into our kitchen and said, "Whoa. I've never seen that before. That's so cool!"

The fact that angels having brown skin stops us in our tracks should give us all pause. I wish I'd noticed all the blonde angels before KD pointed them out. I wish I'd gotten out ahead of this problem—and a thousand others.

But sometimes our kids show us the areas where we need to evolve.

I have found that parents' unresolved issues can rear their ugly heads when we watch our kids navigate their teen and young-adult years. Breakups, for example, are moments when it's really hard to maintain reason and sanity.

To see my kids heartbroken is much harder than I'd expected. I've had my most independent child crawl into my bed. I've listened to stories about their exes and wondered if voodoo might be a good hobby for me to learn.

In these situations, I've turned to friends whose kids are older than mine. Some really helpful advice was to be grateful for the good parts of my kids' first serious relationships, especially if they were healthy, caring starts at love.

The other thing people told me was to be careful what I said about the exes, because there was a very good chance that they wouldn't be gone forever. Sure enough, an orbiting seems to happen with first loves. Your child and their ex might keep circling each other for a few years.

It'll be less awkward for everyone, then, if you haven't put a pox on their house.

There is simply no way to anticipate all the adjustments we'll need to make in response to the specific kids we've been given. We can make ourselves miserable by keeping track of all the things we should have known or didn't see coming. Instead, let's give ourselves and one another credit for the ways we've grown and changed.

Parenting is really hard. Not just for me. Not just for you. For everyone. We're all just doing the best we can with what we've got.

And that's okay.

Write "I'm doing great—this is hard for everyone" or some other encouraging statement in a place where you'll see it regularly. Remind yourself of this when you are convinced that you're the only one botching parenthood.

I often think, "Why didn't they warn us about this stuff at baby showers?" Are there things you wish you'd known before you were in the thick of raising kids? Is it maybe better to learn and grow along with your kids?

CHAPTER 6

Remember that you'll be gone someday, and they'll have each other.

WHEN I WORRY that I don't have the energy or love to care for four kids, I try to remember that it isn't a zero-sum game. I can't give each of our kids the time or energy I could if there were fewer of them, but I have given them one another.

There's something about siblings—confidantes

who remember holidays gone wrong and adventures kept from parents and truths that feel too heavy to carry alone.

Of course, no siblings remember their childhoods the same way. My two younger brothers and I have vastly differing memories and takeaways. My kids are the same way. The big kids act like they grew up without running water while the twins have butlers.

The details matter less than the truth that siblings can protect one another with fierceness—sometimes even from the parents. I feel ashamed to write this, but sometimes my big kids have served as a buffer between me and the twins.

I remember in particular a family-picture day gone wrong. I'd managed to get the four kids presentable and somewhat coordinated (though there was no chance that Bryan and I could also be photo worthy). As my photographer friend started taking pictures of my beautiful children on the riverbank, I noticed that one of the twins was doing a weird smile, like she was poking her front teeth out and intentionally looking bad. I suggested that she "smile normal," which made her cry. So, we went from a weird smile to no smile at all. Thankfully, Caroline sat down on a rock with her and comforted her.

I felt like a real witch . . . but I also wanted to get a Christmas card picture that wasn't terrible, which we eventually got. I'm sure that no one who got our lovely card realized that there had been tears, as well as a really great sibling rescue, moments before the shot.

There's a scene in the movie *Little Miss Sunshine* where the uncle realizes that his sweet niece is in no way prepared for a pageant she is about to enter. She's in way over her head, and he's seriously worried for her precious heart. As she's bombing her wildly inappropriate dance routine, he and the other family members jump on the stage to dance with her.

Being "pageant ready" doesn't really matter in the end. What endures is our duty to not leave anyone alone on the stage. Or the river rocks.

That's what people who love you do.

Of course, it's not always perfect with siblings. Sometimes families need UN level negotiations to arrange holidays. Sometimes siblings fall out, disengage, or just can't handle one another as adults. And oftentimes, caring for aging parents complicates things even more.

But I've always firmly held the belief that being estranged from my siblings isn't an option. I learned this from my mom. She lost her only brother in the Vietnam War. As a result of that trauma, it's been super important to her that my brothers and I value one another. She has one sister, whom I'm very close to. I've watched those two sisters carry each other through grief and joy over the decades.

My brothers are hilarious and have big personalities, but they don't always get along, which is hard because I love them both dearly. Usually, neither of them is right, and they're both right. When they're at odds, I sometimes put a lot of effort and energy into being on good terms with each of them. Other times, though, I don't let their storm take up too much of my headspace. I just wait for it to pass, which it eventually does.

All I know for sure is this: if I had to pick out two brothers from all the boys in the world, I'd choose them every time. But that's the thing about families: we *don't* get to pick. We do, however, get to decide how we'll treat one another as we grow.

The last time Caleb was home from college, I noticed how much he and Caroline gave each other a hard time. There was a lot of teasing and calling out.

It made me realize that they aren't super gentle with each other—in a way that surprises me, because I'm pretty careful with all the kids. It's like they're tough on each other, yet fierce about each other. I'd think twice before I came for either one of them, is what I'm saying.

And that brings me great comfort.

Can you think of a time when a sibling supported you? Call and thank them if possible.

If you have friends with older kids, ask them how they've encouraged sibling sweetness. (For example, I have a friend who picks up the tab anytime her kids meet for dinner.)

CHAPTER 7

Remember that we all make mistakes as parents.

A FRIEND OF mine was crying to her therapist because of something she'd said to her kid. "She will surely end up in therapy!" my friend said.

"Probably," her therapist agreed. "But it won't be because of the things you've said or done. Everyone needs therapy for their own reasons."

So, yes—our kids will probably need therapy.

We have to keep trying anyway.

As parents, we make a lot of mistakes. None of us were properly trained for such an important job. We're thrown curveballs, and we have to adjust. We're learning on the job, and we constantly get new information.

When Caleb came out as gay in tenth grade, I didn't handle it as well as I would have expected. I'm a progressive Christian who had been vocal about LGBTQIA+ rights in the church and world. It was different, though, when it was my own kid.

I was worried for his safety in rural Georgia, so I let fear be the boss of me. If I could, I'd change so many things about that stretch in our lives. But the main thing I'd change is being more of a warrior and less of a mouse.

The how and why of Caleb's coming-out is his story to tell; it's certainly not mine. Suffice it to say, there were some alternate truths and a beautiful boy at the center of it all. It was not a celebratory or a tidy coming-out.

It was more of a roll-out with no master plan and no point person.

My clearest memory of this time was when I was heading up the stairs in the middle of the night to check on Caleb, and I passed Bryan coming back down from doing the same thing. It was like we had a newborn again. In some ways, we did. Caleb was vulnerable, and we didn't know what we were doing.

As that initial vulnerable time passed, we all adjusted to our new normal. I learned new things every day, such as the truth that gay guys share clothes in a way that totally makes sense. (Also that when these relationships end, serious mediation is required to return sweatshirts and ripped jeans to their rightful owners.) I also realized that spend-the-nights would always be complicated.

It was good to finally talk about these new-to-us experiences openly. But after a while, Caleb wondered why we were still talking about them. To him, being gay was *part* of who he was; though maybe not even the most interesting part.

To me, however, it was all a pretty big deal. It might have been a generational difference, but I felt as though an earthquake had hit our house and that it was unrealistic to pretend otherwise.

I even felt it in social situations with other parents. I felt like they were all looking at me, wondering if I knew about Caleb. Granted, I was looking at them, wondering if they knew.

Soon enough, I started to care less and less what other people did or didn't know. I finally realized that if Caleb didn't feel the need to call a press conference, then I didn't either.

Still, I needed to find ways to address this new issue directly. I had a weekly blog where I often shared our family experiences, but instead of writing about Caleb's coming out, I mostly wrote around it that first year. It wasn't my story alone to tell. It would have been a lot to ask a tenth grader to allow his mom to blog about his coming out in real time.

But it was still something I needed to process constantly, so I found other means. I found myself a new therapist. I called my three closest girlfriends to come over one afternoon, and they showed up with dark chocolate, kind words, and a dose of courage. I read books with unsubtle titles like *This Is a Book for Parents of Gay Kids*. I found resources and parenting groups online. I mostly observed without contributing, but I learned so much from seasoned parents of LGBTQIA+ kids. I made the conscious decision to be less fragile and less dramatic.

I also started treating Caleb's relationship with his boyfriend the same way I'd treat any of my kids' serious relationships. I started texting with his boyfriend, and we followed each other on Instagram. I made sure he felt included in activities with our family, such as the Christmas Eve service at our church.

I've gotten some things right and some things terribly wrong.

When Caleb wanted to use a fireman-themed poster, complete with flames, to ask his boyfriend to homecoming, I replied, "Isn't that a little too gay?" I regretted it immediately. I think I was just scared for him to be so very out in small-town Georgia.

I tried to make it up to him by buying them fireman hats. Caroline made the poster for him, just as she'd made a poster for him when he had asked a girl to a previous homecoming. I ordered two coordinating (but not matching) boutonnieres without oversharing to the florist. I took pictures of Caleb and his date and put them on social media. I practiced saying "my son's boyfriend" without any hesitation or apology in my voice.

We became a different kind of family than we'd been before Caleb had come out. Now we're more honest and we're bolder. We're also more careful with one another.

Nonetheless, I didn't handle my son's coming out as well as I wish I had. I think I would have handled it better if it'd happened when he was twenty-five instead of fifteen. But that's not how it unfolded. Instead, it got all swirled in with the time when he needed more space from me, which I now realize is appropriate and healthy for any teenage boy.

We don't get to sketch out the timeline of our kids' discoveries. Life happens when it happens.

Another big mistake we made as parents was imagining that we were prepared for transracial adoption. We passed the home study, and no one raised concerns. But looking back, I recognize that the first Black people to spend the night at our house shouldn't have been our own children. My plan, I think, was to fold the twins into our already existing world—church, schools, friendships—but our world wasn't diverse enough.

I have skin in the game now. But I should have been in the game before we adopted the twins.

Honestly, I'd assumed I was in the game. We went to racial equality marches when we lived in Mississippi. My dad was raised a Quaker, and my parents are tremendously progressive. As cliché as it sounds, I had Black friends.

But none of this is the same as being a mom to children of color. I'm learning by looking around, reading, asking questions, and watching Black moms in particular.

As a family, we've made some changes in the past few years that we could have made sooner. We switched schools and moved into town, where there is more diversity. We seek out mentors and guides who look like the twins, because there is no amount of reading or antiracism training or progressiveness that can teach me what it's like to be a young Black woman walking through life. I'll never know.

I also won't ever know what it's like to be a gay kid in the world, but I have become more of the warrior I wish I'd been six years ago.

I'll keep making mistakes, but I'll also keep trying.

Complete this thought: "I didn't know_____ then, but now I do. And next time, I'll do _____."

What are the areas in which you can show yourself some kindness and grace for past mistakes?

THESE THINGS GO

CHAPTER 8

Stop looking around so much.

MAYBE IT'S BECAUSE we live in a university town, or maybe it's because most parents I know aren't in their twenties, but I am surrounded by some intense parenting. Especially when my kids were little, I'd find myself saying, "Your son plays the violin? Isn't he, like, three? Oh, and a Spanish-immersion Montessori camp? Wow. What a great summer plan."

I'd regularly walk away from conversations with other parents and think, *My kids are so screwed.* My summer plan was to keep everyone alive, which was much harder than it sounds. That was as high as I could aim.

And then there were the times when a grandma would bend down to talk to one of my kids, and I could sense the interrogation coming.

"What do you like to do? Are you a gymnast? Do you play soccer? How about an instrument?" (What is it with the instruments? Are we supposed to be forming a family band?)

"No," I would interrupt. "She likes to jump on the trampoline with her sisters."

Then I'd panic. How will she ever get a job? She has no skills. Am I only preparing her for circus work?

"Isn't she, like, six?" my husband would say on his way to jump with them.

Great. Now we'll all be a circus family.

Jealousy likes to make an appearance when we look around and feel like everyone else knows what they are doing. I am baffled and even a little green when I see pictures of moms I know finishing marathons or doing relay runs across state lines. Or when I see pictures of families climbing mountains and wrestling bears or whatever. I wonder how they found shoes for everyone to wear before it got dark.

Our regular life with four kids felt adventure-some enough, without adding anything epic on top of it. I feel like weekends flew by for us, with sports and theater practices. Some Sundays, all six of us just weren't presentable enough for church. We usually went anyway. We have a terrifying Easter picture where the kids look precious, but I look like I've just been released from the hospital.

Jealousy can be useful sometimes, of course. It can teach us something; it can provide clues about what we long for when we see something in others. Other times, I am so envious of easy, breezy families that I lose sight of how awesome my own family is. It's not a good look on me.

Even though jealousy often likes to jump in the car, we should never let it drive. And here's why: Jealousy doesn't have all the information. Jealousy doesn't always have our kids' best interests in mind.

In addition to having processing speed learning disabilities, our sweet Elizabeth had strabismus (or eye-turning) in both eyes, probably from being born so premature. Learning to read was a chal-lenge for both twins, but Elizabeth had the extra challenge of literally seeing double. It's really hard to read when your eyes struggle to track the words. We tried vision therapy for several years and had her wear tiny, pink bifocal glasses with diamonds on the side.

It didn't seem fair that she had so many challenges. Why was everything so much harder for her? I was so jealous of the moms who were already looking for chapter books for their young kids. I wasn't gracious.

It turns out I was just being impatient. We found a great surgeon at Emory who was able to correct both of Elizabeth's eyes. She learned to read when the time was right, with the help of some really patient teachers. By fifth grade, she was pumped to go with me to the bookstore and library. And now I have to move stacks of books to get to her bed. She's my biggest reader.

It wasn't those other moms' fault that Elizabeth couldn't read with the rest of her class. It wasn't Elizabeth's fault or mine. It wasn't anybody's fault. It just wasn't time yet.

Sometimes our kids catch up, and that's a reason for exuberant celebration. Sometimes, though, catching up just isn't possible. I've seen this with friends whose kids are on the autism spectrum. These kids can struggle mightily with social cues and making friends—and a mom can struggle mightily if she assumes she's a failure just because her kid doesn't want to invite the whole class to their birthday party.

What if, instead, we measured our kids according to their own little clocks? What if we adjusted our expectations and followed our kids' pace? What if we put those chapter books away for a while, or invited two kids instead of twenty to a birthday party? What if we celebrated the small steps instead of expecting great leaps?

Elizabeth's first-grade teacher had only two rules: "Be kind. Work hard."

I think we parents rock the "work hard" part, whether we work outside the home or put our house back together after the morning storm. It's the "be kind" part we could work on a little. As in, be kind to ourselves. And that includes not looking around so much.

There's a reason why coaches always remind swimmers to "swim in your own lane." They aren't talking about staying in your lane physically—the ropes handle that part. They're talking about staying in your own lane mentally and emotionally. They're talking about not comparing ourselves to others. Coaches know that looking around messes with our heads and slows us down.

I promise that we'll all swim best if we stay in our own lanes. And it won't hurt to remind one another that it's a long race.

When are you especially susceptible to comparing your family to other families? Around the holidays? At school events? On the athletic fields? How can you center yourself so you don't despair in these moments?

What makes your family unique? Can you embrace that?

CHAPTER 9

Stop treating your kids like walking report cards.

NOBODY DOUBTS THAT you love your kids to the moon and back; we all know that they carry our hearts out into the world every single time they leave the house. But it's really hard to know if we're doing a good job. There are no grades or report cards for moms.

I especially struggled with this when I left church work and became a full-time, stay-at-home mom. Suddenly, I was no longer getting performance reviews or feedback on my programs or any other data about the effects of how I spent my days. I wanted reassurance that I'd made the right choice and that my kids would be okay, but a mom can't really ask her kids for a performance review. (Can you imagine how drunk with power that would make them?)

How was I supposed to know if I was doing it "right" or not?

I can't be the first mom in history who's looked for outside validation, especially when in a new stage of life with kids. Instead of realizing that we're probably doing okay, many of us become convinced that we're blowing it.

In our desperation, then, we turn our kids into walking report cards. We convince ourselves that our kids' accomplishments and milestones are reflections of our own mothering abilities.

Is my kid doing well in school? Do they have friends? Are they healthy?

What if the answer to these questions is no, despite doing our absolute best with these precious humans? What if our kids aren't thriving—does that mean we aren't doing a good job?

It can be even more problematic if the answer to these questions is always "YES!" I know the smugness of being a parent of a kid who's doing well. It feels good when your kid is hitting the mark.

It's really tempting to pat yourself on the back when, in truth, you had very little to do with their success. Some kids just luck out genetically and have brains that are good at school. I can promise you that we read to all our kids, not just the one who ended up in the gifted program.

It's not good for anyone if we moms treat our kids as walking report cards. It's too much for a toddler or a teen to carry, and it's too arbitrary of a yardstick to have any real merit.

Caroline was a distance runner in high school and had the privilege of being offered a spot on the University of Georgia's cross-country and track and field teams. She was in the local paper, and her high school hosted a signing day. It was a big deal.

And then, in the middle of her sophomore year, she quit the team.

Bryan, who'd been a college runner himself, took her decision in stride. But I did not handle it as well as I would have expected. I struggled as if *I* had been the one to make a big life change.

It wasn't as though I'd been living through her, exactly. I had no desire to race fast people. I'm not an athlete. But I loved that she was. I loved all the UGA gear and all the opportunities she got. I loved that I could watch her do her thing even after she'd graduated from high school.

Most importantly, I loved what her making the team meant to our family. It felt like a victory of sorts. *It felt like we'd finally gotten something right.*

And then it all just vanished. Poof.

Why did I have so much trouble? I think I was trying to turn her accomplishments into my own validation. It wasn't until she'd quit the team that I realized how often I'd "mentioned" that my daughter was an athlete. Or how often I'd wear a UGA track and field sweatshirt at yoga and mention that she ran for the university. No one had been asking.

I had to check myself. I reached out to some moms who'd been in similar situations. One friend from church had a son who'd quit his college soccer team. She was so reassuring. She'd been through it not only as a mom, but also as an academic advisor. Apparently, many sophomore athletes throw in the towel. She reminded me that being a Division I athlete is like holding a full-time job alongside all the expected classwork; kids who don't absolutely love their sport shouldn't keep doing it.

When my daughter was thinking about quitting, I asked her, "What will you do instead of running?" She had a whole, big, long list. "Study abroad, join a sorority, do more entrepreneurial stuff." You know, have a life. Even though she stayed at UGA, it's like she was at a different college. It was definitely the right choice for her and what she wanted during her college years.

Once the dust settled, I was happy for her. And I was humbled.

It's also been humbling to have kids who struggle in school. As someone who used education as a vehicle to get from one place to the next, having three kids with learning disabilities sent me into a downward spiral.

Will they ever be able to read? Will they finish high school? Will they be employable? Am I doing something wrong? (Yes, yes, yes, and no.)

I've shifted my expectations over the years. With the twins, I do a celebration dance anytime their standardized test scores are in the average range. I want to throw a party for every teacher who helps them get to "grade level." They both have IEPs and will continue to struggle with school. But man, are they trying.

When I remember to stop panicking, my heart softens a bit, and I realize how hard their brains have to work just to keep up at school. I'm more compassionate about their mood swings and frustrations.

There's a line in the musical *Hamilton* that says, "The fact that you are alive is a miracle. Just stay alive. It should be enough." I try to remember what a feat of survival it is that the twins are still here. Anything on top of that is just gravy.

The fact that I'm still here, as mom to these four kids, should be enough too.

What expectations for your kids have you had to adjust to fit with the reality of your life?

Setting aside your kids' accomplishments, what have you *accomplished that makes you feel proud? What personal history can you draw from when your confidence is lacking?*

CHAPTER 10

Stop disappearing into your kids.

IN COLLEGE, I had a literature professor who, one day, shared something very important with our class. After a discussion about a short story, she leaned against her desk and said, "I'll tell you something that has taken me countless hours and thousands upon thousands of dollars to learn in therapy. Here it is: I am not my mother."

We were all very quiet. Maybe the other students were quiet because they were awed. I don't know. I just clearly remember thinking, "Can you get your money back . . . ?" Not being one's mother seemed pretty obvious to my twenty-year-old self.

But now I fully understand her epiphany.

I thought of her when I was sitting in therapy a year ago. My therapist asked how I was doing, and I gave her extensive updates on every single one of my kids.

Eventually, she stopped me and said, "We're here to talk about *you*. How are *you*?"

I stared back at her, blinking. I had no idea how I was.

In that moment, I realized, "I am not my kids."

I'm sure this seems obvious to many of you, but I forget that I am more than a mom. Often.

When it's easier for me to talk about my kids than myself, I know I've neglected my essential self. The way this shows up in my life is when someone, like my therapist, asks how I am, and I respond with "Let me tell you about my kids instead."

I know there are plenty of moms out there who have healthy boundaries with their kids and don't struggle with this. But I also know a lot of moms, myself included, who have to fight their tendency to disappear into their kids.

It took Caroline quitting college athletics for me to make some long-overdue adjustments. I realized that I needed more hobbies than just watching my kids do their stuff. I needed to find some joy and fun of my own.

Once I'd decided I needed more fun in my life, I made a list (I'm so fun! I make lists!) of things I'd been wanting to do or things I could try that weren't directly tied to being a mom. Surely, I could think of some fun things to do outside of my family.

I wrote, "That sounds fun . . ." at the top of my notepad, then waited for the inspiration to flow.

It turned out to be a real head-scratcher. I literally walked around asking myself, "What sounds fun to you, Anna?"

I looked around—not to compare and judge but to simply see what other people did for fun. I remembered that my dad doesn't wait for someone to give him permission to try new things. There's a lot to admire about him, but the way he's rocked retirement is at the top of the list. He makes beautiful bowls at the woodworking guild. He starts pickleball programs in his community. He grows roses to take to friends and bakes amazing sourdough bread. Surely, I could learn from his zest for life.

Even with that inspiration, it took me at least a

week to come up with some ideas. At the top of my list was horseback riding, which I love. I only rarely rode as a kid, and I'd only done it on vacation as an adult. So, I asked around, found someone who offered lessons nearby, and made plans to meet her at her farm.

When I told Bryan and the kids about my new adventure, one of my twins commented that she'd always wanted to ride and asked if she could come too. Then Bryan added that we have friends with horses and that we could all go out to their farm together.

"This isn't a group project!" I practically yelled.

My hunch that I needed something just for *me* was confirmed in that moment.

Remember when I told you about my "Soul Care for Moms" workshop and how the moms with the youngest kids cry because they have no idea what they love? It totally makes sense that they've disappeared into the demands of motherhood during those hands-on years. Most of us do. It takes a lot to keep these people alive.

The danger is in staying in that all-consuming

place long past when our kids actually need us all the time. (At least that's the danger for me. I tend to hover and fuss and panic, regardless of my kids' ages.)

There's a bit of a danger, too, when we get super invested in our kids' successes and activities as they grow. We've all seen this play out on social media with moms who brag all the time. (Or wear their UGA track and field gear to yoga.) In most cases, this works itself out. Those kids eventually go on to have their own lives, and those moms go on too.

The moms I worry about the most are the ones whose kids are truly hurting, at any age. Those moms take on their kids' struggles as their full identities.

I've been there before. During a crisis or a difficult stretch, we moms are typically the ones who find therapists and tutors and school resources.

When times are tough, our kids do need us. Intensely. But in most cases, they won't always need us at that level.

Our kids are more than their struggles; we are more than moms of kids in crisis.

Now that I have more interests outside of my kids, I can recognize how I was hiding behind them. I let myself get caught up in their successes, their struggles, and their everyday in-betweens. I know I'm not doing great when I've burrowed into my kids. It's not healthy for any of us.

Kids move out. That's what they are supposed to do. We can send them out the door with blessings and prayers, or we can claw and grasp at their legs. Either way, they are going. It's best for everyone involved if we let them go graciously—and make sure we have some form of a life outside of them.

My mom always told me that her job was to work herself out of the job of being a parent. And she succeeded.

I still need my mom sometimes, but not like a child needs a parent. I now want her in my life as someone who always has my back, who can help me recalibrate, who wants what is best for me even when it isn't easy for her. My mom had no interest in being my friend when I was growing up; she was decisively my mom. Now, she's both.

I also learned the importance of working

ourselves out of this job from a mom at Target. Her ten-year-old kid had a walker and had gotten turned around on the slight decline between the automatic doors and the parking lot. He kept calling out for her. She kept shaking her head and telling him to turn his walker.

I was panicked, watching, but I noticed that her other kids didn't look concerned.

The boy very slowly turned his walker; then his face lit up. "I did it, Mom!"

She smiled and said, "I knew you could."

I'd wanted her to carry him and his walker to their car. But instead, she'd prepared him for his future life without her.

At the end of that one therapy session, my therapist quoted Kahlil Gibran: "Your children are not your children. They are the sons and daughters of Life's longing for itself."

I'm not quite at that level, but I do know for certain that I am not my kids.

I think that's progress.

How do you respond when someone asks, "How are you doing?" Practice responding with sentences that start with "I . . ." instead of "We . . ."

Make a list of something fun you want to do every month for the next year. (Start with relatively inexpensive and easy-to-accomplish things. Big, fancy, expensive events or trips aren't necessary for this to be meaningful for you!)

Stop thinking you owe everyone an explanation.

THIS SOUNDS COUNTERINTUITIVE, but the more challenges I've faced with my kids, the smaller my circle has gotten. I don't feel isolated, especially, but I do feel cautious.

I think we, as moms, are encouraged to have a whole big "tribe" to help us raise our kids. It works for some families. And I certainly feel like I have church folks and online communities and former teachers cheering my children on. No doubt. But there are only a handful of friends who know everything that is happening in my house.

We all know people who view information as a commodity to be traded. And this can be incredibly hurtful if what they are sharing is precious and private to your family.

If you aren't absolutely sure that the people around you—friends or family—are on your kids' side, then you don't owe them information. You might even decide that you don't have time or energy to keep people whom you don't trust in your life.

Of course, there are certain people in our lives that we must be around for a thousand different reasons. But you don't have to give them your whole heart, is what I'm saying. Especially if they've already shown you that they are careless.

I was in an upsetting social situation right after my girls were diagnosed with learning disabilities. A mom I've struggled to get along with over the years invited us over for a summer cookout. She knew what we were going through with our girls and how worried I was that school would always be a challenge for my kids.

Nonetheless, she kept talking throughout the dinner about how smart and gifted her kids were.

She would not stop. If she hadn't known about my family's current distress, it would have been simply obnoxious. But this felt cruel.

Hope springs eternal, so I decided to give her another chance when she suggested we meet up again. I thought maybe she would be kinder the next time we saw her. Just in case she wasn't, though, I decided that the best way to get through the evening was to make up a drinking game, where I'd take a sip of my wine every time she mentioned "gifted."

I don't drink very often, so I had to abandon the game after I heard about "gifted preschool" and "gifted testing" and "gifted classes." It went on all through dinner. I hadn't been imagining it the first time; she was really into her family's "giftedness." My husband and I were very quiet throughout the evening, but that didn't stop the gifted talk. Apparently, as gifted as her family was, she hadn't been gifted with social awareness.

I decided that we didn't have to subject ourselves to those braggy monologues anymore. I've gradually backed away from that mom. I don't think she has the capacity to be kind to my kids (or to me) regarding their struggles.

It's a call I get to make.

I started to sense the importance of being careful with my kids' information almost as soon as we adopted the twins. There are parts of their story that even my parents and my biological children don't know—parts that are just sad and not especially helpful. There are parts of their story that aren't mine to share. Full stop.

There are also parts of their story that I don't feel obligated to share with every person who asks me an invasive question at a swim meet or in the grocery store. Sometimes, people ask because they're thinking about adopting or because they personally know people who are foster parents. Other times, people are just nosy.

You wouldn't believe the questions random people ask adoptive parents. It's *wild*! I have friends who adopted a beautiful little girl from China. They got so tired of being asked "How much did she cost?" that they framed it in car terms: "Less than a Subaru, more than a Honda."

I've been asked if the twins' "real mother" was on drugs and if they are "real sisters." Whenever this happened when the twins were very little, I wanted to say to people, "They can hear you, you know?" Now that the twins are older, people sometimes pose these invasive questions directly to them, which has led to some very interesting encounters. I often remind the twins that they don't have to tell more than they are comfortable sharing.

As a family, we've gotten better at discerning when people have a personal investment in our family and when they're just digging for gossip. I realize we stand out as a family, and I want to err on the side of being gracious, especially if the people asking seem well intentioned. I want to be helpful— like an unofficial ambassador for adoption—but not at the risk of making my kids feel unsafe or like a circus act.

Once, an airport-shuttle driver asked if the twins were from Haiti. "No," Bryan answered, barely pausing as he loaded our luggage. The one word response was pretty curt, in my opinion, but Bryan felt like he'd answered the question adequately. He's better at just stating the facts.

This awareness about oversharing has helped shape the focus of this book. My purpose of writing this book is less about how to address specific challenges your kids are facing and more about how you can navigate them as a mom. Because a lot of the skills transfer.

Case in point, most of you reading this book haven't adopted children who are a different race than you; children who have a story that must be guarded. But you still need to know how to respond when a teacher or stranger really digs in about your kids. You still need to know how you—and your kids—can respond to invasive questions with decent manners but also with strong boundaries. You still need to know where to draw the line between being helpful to other families and jeopardizing the privacy of your own.

I know we're all just doing our best and trying to piece together parenting practices on the fly, but every kid is vulnerable in some way. They all need our help discerning who can be trusted with their precious hearts. Whether our kids are struggling or soaring, they need adults in their lives who champion them and adore them.

Eventually, I know my kids will find their own circles and create their own families. But in the meantime, I intend to make sure my circle and my family are as safe and affirming as they can possibly be.

Whom do you trust with your stories? And with your kids' stories? (They might be different people.)

Before you share something about your kids, ask yourself if you would say it if they were standing beside you. (I'm still working on this.)

CHAPTER 12

Stop agreeing to things you wish hadn't been asked of you.

I'M A FIFTY-ONE-YEAR-OLD woman who has only recently started asking myself, "What do *you* want to do, Anna? Do you want to go to that?" when I receive an email request or when I'm working on my calendar. I usually know the answer in my gut.

If it's something I rush to sign up for because I'm eager to help, then that's a good sign. Saying yes to it is a good choice. But if I sign up only because someone made me feel guilty, then it won't go well.

In other words, if it's something I wish I hadn't been asked to do, then I should say no.

I've spent a lot of years saying yes to things people asked of me and then resenting having to do them. That's not fair to anyone.

I suspect there are families in our community who think we don't pull our weight. At least there are some who find us unreliable. Sometimes I have to ignore the guilt I feel about not being able to do everything. I have to remind myself that most of these things are not mandatory.

When I'm trying to decide what commitments our family will make, I often say, "We just can't pull that off." What I mean is that the energy and time required will put us at a deficit.

For instance, if I'm thinking straight, I can look at our calendar and say, "Signing my child up for a gymnastics team that requires us to travel will end badly." Or, "Yes, we could possibly make it to math night at multiple schools, but at what cost? If half of us arrive in tears and are exhausted the next day, was that worth it?"

Of course, it's best to figure out such things *before* you commit to a team or a project. Ghosting on people who are counting on you feels rotten for everyone.

I know a family who made a spreadsheet detailing the weekends their high school students would still be living at home. Some of those weekends were already filled with work and other obligations. The spreadsheet helped them decide whether to commit to new things.

If your kid will be living at home for only fifty more weekends, and thirty of those are already full . . . do you really want to spend the remaining twenty weekends breathlessly racing between unnecessary activities?

When the poet Mary Oliver died a few years ago, I noticed a flurry of people posting a quote from one of her most famous poems: "Tell me, what it is you plan to do with your one wild and precious life?"

At first glance, it seems like a call to cram in as much as possible. But then I remembered that Mary Oliver spent her days observing and writing about nature. She sought astonishment in quiet places. The poem isn't a call to overcommitment or to efficiency; it's a call to live more deeply and more intentionally.

I used to think that being a good steward of my time meant using each moment efficiently. Now, I'd like to not make the people around me miserable with impossible expectations.

In the end, we get to shape these families of ours.

I have a strong sense of who I want us to be as a family. The last thing I want is for my kids to look back on their childhoods as a sort of forced march.

One of my core values is that my kids grow up to become fierce companions and advocates for one another. Time spent laughing in the kitchen moves us toward that possibility. So does time playing basketball in the driveway.

While we can't put these "at home" moments on a college application, they do shape our kids. We need some uncommitted time and space to just be a family. To me, those moments aren't optional.

They're sacred.

Before you make a big decision about your family's time, take the time to sit with your options and see how each one makes you feel in your gut or heart or head. How has your body let you know the best choice in the past?

Did you listen?

I love the show Schitt's Creek, *and I cackle every time the character David Rose ungraciously declines an invitation or request from his family. Some of my favorites are "I'm trying very hard not to connect with people right now" and "I won't be doing any of that" and "That's a hard pass." Do you ever wish you could say something like that? What would your catchphrase be?*

CHAPTER 13

Stop expecting your kids to be delightful, reasonable, and nice to live with.

Both of my teenagers have been madder than usual at me lately. My best guess is that they're mostly angry that I won't let them do everything they want to do.

More times than I can count, I've turned to my husband after some unexpected dramatic episode and said, "What in the world was that?" It's like the twins get taken over by aliens, but then they're fine ten minutes later. It's dizzying.

There's a weird vibe in our house that I've struggled to identify. Is it like a psych ward? Or maybe the Upside Down from *Stranger Things*?

Finally, I've put my finger on it: *toddlers*. My teenagers remind me of toddlers—but with raging hormones and mood swings.

It reminds me of the time when one of my toddlers was prescribed a steroid. I called a girlfriend who is a nurse for advice. "Oh boy—get ready," she said. "A toddler on steroids is like living with a squirrel on crack." A hormonal teenager is kind of the same.

Good times.

I'm sure a lot of experts have written about this, but here are five ways I've realized that toddlers and teenagers are very similar.

1. *Their meltdowns come out of nowhere.* Neither age group will say, "I'm overwhelmed. Can you help me process these changes in my life?" Instead, they will lose it over shoes being tight or smoothies being lumpy. Whenever this happens, there's a good

chance that they're simply overstimulated and need more sleep. Soothing baths can also help both toddlers and teenagers.

2. *They resist basic safety and reasonable boundaries.* I've read in multiple books that both toddlers and teenagers need boundaries and that they "secretly crave them." Yet both age groups act like we're vengeful for having rules that are simply designed to keep these erratic and unpredictable humans out of traffic and out of jail.

It's enough to make us parents think we're doing something wrong. But trust me—we are right to enforce our rules. We actually do know more than they do. We really do.

3. *It's not personal.* When we first moved to Athens, I signed Caroline up for a toddler gymnastics class. Caleb was a newborn in a snuggie, and I was trying to keep up with Caro. (Why did we ever even try to leave the house?) At one point, she got mad and hit me. I was mortified. I didn't know these other moms, and here was my kid, walloping me. A generous mom came over to me as I was packing up to leave. "There isn't a mom here who hasn't been hit or kicked by their child," she said. "It's not you. It's them."

All of us moms get pushback from toddlers and teenagers alike. The pushback just changes as our kids get older. Obviously, no one is hitting me anymore, but my teenagers make their displeasure known in other ways. With teens, we moms have to get tougher so we can handle their anger and disgust.

4. *They're not babies.* Toddlers need less care than babies, and teenagers are practically adults. So if you're still babying either age group, you might need to check yourself.

This one hurts to write. When I feel disconnected from my kids emotionally, I turn to physical care as a way to show that I love them to the moon and back. Wanting to do more for them isn't necessarily a bad thing, but I know it's reached the unhealthy point when my kids start treating me like an underperforming and disappointing personal assistant. Teenagers can feed themselves and take care of their possessions. It's good practice for life.

5. *It's our job to keep them safe and ourselves sane; everything else that happens during these years is a bonus.* We're not here to make friends with either our toddlers or our teenagers. We can't expect them to thank us or praise us for keeping them alive and

well. We can't expect them to be delightful, reasonable, and nice to live with.

One neurobiologist described teenage brains as "Ferraris with weak brakes." As parents, we need to be their brakes. It's not fun, but it's not forever. We must pace ourselves, fellow parents, and try to not get swept up in the hysterics.

But here's the good news: both toddlers and teenagers do settle down eventually. In the case of teenagers, they go off to college and aren't mad at you all the time. If you're super lucky, they become delightful.

Now that you're a parent, have you realized that maybe your parents weren't *the dumbest people on the planet after all? Consider letting them know how you feel and thanking them for not giving up on you when you were a teenager.*

What kind of support would help you when you are "being the brakes" for your teenagers? Or if you still have little ones, are there any lessons you've learned that you can carry forward as they grow up?

MAYBE

WE'LL DO OUR BEST GOING FORWARD

CHAPTER 14

Start developing a new mom uniform.

One spring day when my twins were five years old, I walked out of the child psychologist's office and thought, "I'm going to need a great pair of boots." I'd just learned that the twins were struggling with some significant developmental delays and learning disabilities. I needed a new uniform that would fortify me for the new tasks ahead.

The other thing I needed was a new vocabulary. *Processing speed*, *neurodevelopmental*, and other terms were thrown around. Parents of kids with learning disabilities are their own subculture, with their own language. Now, I know exactly what people mean when they say, "We're moving through the tiers, trying to keep her in the least restrictive environment. Her MAP scores qualified her for EIP. In the spring, we can look at a 504, but an IEP would require more testing."

I also needed to make a new rule for myself: whenever I have meetings with teachers and administrators, I have to keep my shit together. I can't advocate for my kids if I'm blubbering or can't catch my breath. So I tell myself I will not cry until I get to the car. Sometimes I have to run through the parking lot, but I wait until I'm in that safe space.

I need to be a different kind of mom for the twins than I've been for my other children. This mom has to be tougher. I have to fortify myself so I can handle the life I actually have—not the one I imagined when I first became a mom.

Hence, the boots.

This new uniform also helps me to be more compassionate, starting with myself.

Several Februarys ago, I was at the pediatrician's office twice in one week—because I have four kids and it was winter. I was filling out the registration form, explaining the reason for our visit and how long the symptoms had been present. Then I noticed a question I'd never contemplated before: "Does anything make it better or worse?"

It got me thinking about my own life. Most winters, I struggle with sadness, yet somehow it still sneaks up on me every February. I take medicine and go to counseling, but I hate that this still happens to me. If I could, I'd trade my brain with any passing stranger in the hopes that theirs has the ability to sleep, manage their crying, and not take the weather personally.

I've told a few friends about my "brain trade" fantasy and they do not like this idea at all. Their faces look very concerned, and they say things like, "But I love your brain. You wouldn't be Anna with a different brain." I guess this brain and I are partnered for life.

So, what makes my depression better and what makes it worse?

Gray, rainy days make it worse. Taking quick pictures of colorful things in the course of my day makes it better.

Not sleeping well and then drinking too much coffee and not enough water makes it worse. Eating more than just peanut butter toast makes it better.

Deciding that I have no right to feel sad because I have a wonderful life makes it worse. Asking my friend in Florida if it's sunny at her house and then inviting myself to visit the next week makes it better.

Too much social media makes it worse. Prayer and music and flowers and yoga make it better.

Dwelling on all the ways I'm letting people down makes it worse. Pulling out my calendar and planning things like attending UGA basketball games with the twins, walks with friends, and lunch with Bryan makes it better. (Just now, I stopped writing so I could text a friend and ask to meet up this week. I'll be glad that I did.)

Anything that carries even a hint of forward momentum makes it better.

This is what the new uniform is all about—being more compassionate, accepting help, and doing my best to move forward.

One particular morning—when one twin was late for school and the other was super grumpy, when it was raining, when people had coughs, and when everything seemed hard—I looked at our life and thought, "This is a lot, Anna. Most people wouldn't delight in this. You are okay. They are okay. Just keep swimming. Also, take your meds, exercise, don't disappear on people, get some sun when you can, and try not to scare the children."

Instead of berating myself for being high maintenance, I've learned that moving myself up on my own priority list is pretty necessary to get through this. It's just a bit of an episode that needs my attention. I wouldn't judge someone else for needing some time to manage their autoimmune flare-up. I wouldn't demand that someone recovering from pneumonia have their best month ever.

I just need a minute to catch my breath before I can get back in the game. It won't take forever.

The boots are a great start.

What makes you feel fortified to handle the life you actually have—not the one you wish you had? Do you need a uniform, armor, or a superhero costume?

Have you had experiences as a mom that could be helpful to moms newer to the game? For example, several local moms have helped me navigate the world of learning disabilities and academic accommodations. Even small encouragements can make a big difference to moms who are entering new and scary situations!

CHAPTER 15

Start acting like a pool wall.

It's TOUGH TO hit that sweet spot of parenthood. We need to care but not be overbearing. We need to invest in our kids but not overinvest. We need to be involved but not be helicopters or bulldozers.

It's impossible, really. Especially with teenagers and college-age kids. They're doing the important work of learning to trust themselves. They're working hard to make their lives fully their own. They're making big decisions that will affect their futures.

Figuratively and literally, they're driving the car, and you're just along for the ride.

The image I'm finding most helpful lately comes from Lisa Damour's *Untangled: Guiding Teenage*

Girls through the Seven Transitions into Adulthood. Her suggestion is that we should become pool walls for our kids.

Sometimes our kids need to rest on us—and we need to be sturdy enough for that. Sometimes they need to push off of us—and we need to be sturdy enough for that as well.

As our kids get older, we need them to keep telling us stuff, and they need us to keep listening.

At this point, my young-adult kids no longer need my permission, and they aren't really seeking my approval. That means that anything they tell me is bonus—whether it's about their adventures or their relationships or their friends.

I'm doing my best to figure out how to keep them talking. A few years ago, I asked a friend how she kept her older kids talking to her instead of shutting her out.

"I remain as calm as humanly possible," she said. "My dad was a loud, scary guy, and he didn't get told stuff. He missed some pretty big things happening in our house because it was easier for everyone if he didn't know."

Our reactions as parents really matter.

I myself am not too worried about being the loud, scary guy. Rather, I tend to be the fragile, overreacting mom. She doesn't get told things either.

On more than one occasion, I've had conversations with my kids that make me want to run out of the house, screaming with my hair on fire. I need to work on my poker face when they tell me something that's normal for them but hard for me to hear. To name just a few topics: running away from controlling partners—and also from hard drugs; maintaining a bikini line; hiding fake IDs; using condoms; eating too much ice cream when you're lonely; losing too much weight in a few months; figuring out the difference between depression and normal teenage tiredness; navigating what counts as porn; not answering emotional booty calls; trying to be less embarrassing white people when we're at the twins' new high school; sharing too much online; sharing too little with siblings.

The whole "big kids, big problems" cliché is true.

When my kids tell me these things, I don't run away screaming, but I often have to back my teary self out of the room because I'm falling apart. I tend to go outside and say, "This isn't about you, Anna."

I remind myself that my kids aren't reckless or wild—nor are they risk-averse, middle-aged scaredy-cats like me. They're young, energetic, and full of life. There are bound to be missteps and mistakes. I also remind myself that loving my kids doesn't mean loving everything they're doing—which is fortunate, since they make some very questionable decisions.

Once I'm sturdier and calmer, I go back inside. "My brain just needed a minute to catch up," I say. "But I really want you to keep telling me stuff."

My poker face isn't the only thing I need to work on. When I'm anxious about what I'm hearing from my kids, I tend to jump in with unsolicited advice. Of course, my solutions favor the safest option, not necessarily my kids' best interests.

This rarely ends well.

Part of becoming an adult is dealing with the consequences of our decisions. I don't do my kids any favors by running interference for them.

Besides, the last thing they need is me making their tough decisions even tougher. If you've ever had to make a difficult decision—whether or not to stay in a relationship, a job, or a town—then you probably know how strong outside pressures can be. It takes a tremendous amount of strength and a burst of bravery to bust out of the expectations holding you down.

My brother had a friend growing up who went by the name Spoda. This nickname came from the fact that, according to his mother, he never did what he was "spoda" do.

I sometimes feel like none of my kids are doing what they are "spoda" do. This is usually a sign that I'm not paying attention to who they actually are and will be. Instead, I'm trying to control who I want them to be. And I'm often dead wrong.

I am the most judgy when I am the most insecure.

Many of us have the idea that if other people do what they're "spoda" do, maybe the world will be less scary. But a small life and a fearful heart aren't what we want for the people we love.

I've found that it helps to work on some of your own stuff. I highly recommend therapy if you need help processing. One way or another, it's good to work your unresolved issues out on your own and not out on your kids. That's messy, unhelpful, and sometimes damaging. If I can help it, I like to avoid sloshing my crazy over onto my kids.

It's not easy, though. I regularly wonder, "What fresh hell is this?" when one of my kids has some kind of meltdown in the family room. I usually figure out a solution or at least a temporary fix, but then someone else loses it.

These are the kind of days that make me certain that I'm not hardy enough for this life we've built. Or that I'm at least not properly trained.

One paradox of motherhood that I've struggled with is how intense my feelings are about my kids. I adore them and think about them 24/7. I also sometimes want them all to get the hell out of my house so I can think straight for one hot minute. All this can be true at the exact same time. It's confusing for me and probably for them too.

But I'm doing my best. Being a mom has been a twenty-three-year-long lesson in humility and growth.

At times, I've expected my family to hit the bull's-eye on an archery target. My understanding of how a life should look is sometimes way too small.

But each time I've needed to learn something new because of a change in our family, I've moved the bull's-eye zone out a ring or two. I've grown as a person from learning about gender and sexuality, systemic racism, learning disabilities, health issues of preemie babies, and from hard conversations with older teenagers. By necessity—and sometimes reluctantly—I've broadened my ideas about what a good life looks like. I no longer think we're "spoda" hit the bull's-eye.

Lately, I've decided that just not hitting anyone else with our arrow is a worthy goal.

My kids are growing, changing human beings— not robots. So they're unpredictable? I guess I am too. They're irritating? I probably am too. They don't do what they are "spoda" do? Very few of us do.

I want my kids' paths to be as smooth as possible, but that's not how life works. Wanting them to have a life free of suffering isn't reasonable; inevitably, they will get hurt. Being able to stand beside them is the best I can hope for as their mom.

When Caleb came out as gay in high school, I rushed into mom-management mode. I wanted to protect him and keep him safe.

"I don't know how to guide him through this," I remember saying to a friend.

"Is he asking you to guide him . . . ?" she kindly questioned.

Information isn't always an invitation.

This was his journey; I was blessed that he'd included me at all.

Our kids need to feel accepted enough to be real with us. We can be one of the few safe spaces where they don't have to curate their lives to maintain an image. At the end of the day, we all want to be truly seen and still loved.

There are times, of course, when it feels like it would be easier to put our heads in the sand and *not* know some of these hard things about our kids. But ignoring or avoiding the hard stuff only leaves our kids to deal with these situations alone.

It also keeps us from truly knowing our kids. We need to see and hear and love who our kids actually are. We can't just pretend they're some version of the kid we want them to be. That's not really love. That's projection and idealization. That's making our kids' lives all about us.

I want my kids to know I can handle their hard things—these very hard, very real things they're struggling with as they make their way to adulthood. As parents, we get to bear witness to who our kids once were, observe who they currently are, and catch glimpses of who they're becoming.

My therapist is teaching me to say, "I love you and I trust you to make good choices" to my college-age kids. I say it even when I don't quite mean it—yet. I say it even when I'm certain they can hear me rolling my eyes over the phone.

I say it because I need to work myself out of this job of motherhood. I say it because I want it to be true. I say it because I need to practice trusting my kids. I say it because I want them to believe in themselves.

"I love you and I trust you to make good choices" feels like a prayer for their future selves. It's a reminder that they've been prepping for this race their whole lives, and it's a releasing of the baton so they can now sprint away with it.

None of us can predict the future or know what issues our teenagers and young adults will face. But we can shore up our reserves and firm up our walls so we can help them when they need us.

No matter what they're facing, they need reassurance that we're here in case they need to rest against us, before they inevitably push off again.

Think of the times you've been a safe place for your kids to rest—and give yourself credit for those moments.

Do you have a pool wall for yourself?

CHAPTER 16

Start seeing through a new lens.

THERE IS NO doubt in my mind that adopting Black twin daughters has given me a new lens through which I view the world. As a white mom, I see the details of our daily life differently than I did before.

For example, in the county where we lived for twenty years, there are acres and acres of cotton fields. Every fall, I regularly saw families standing in the cotton fields at sunset, taking pictures to be used for Christmas cards or graduation announcements. Often, the families were all dressed in white.

I get it. Cotton is a beautiful crop in the fall. White cotton above dark stems make for a beautiful backdrop.

Nonetheless, every time I saw a cotton field photo session, I'd think, *Nope. Our family is definitely not doing that.*

The problem isn't cotton. The problem is that there is a long and complicated history in the American South regarding cotton. It's hard for me to look at a cotton field and not think of the generations of enslaved people who were forced to work in those fields. To traipse my Black kids out into a cotton field to take pictures would be ignorant at best and cruel at worst.

There are other small ways I see the world differently now. I notice who speaks at worship services. I notice who has access to the microphone at events. I notice when Black people don't make eye contact with me when I'm out with the twins. I notice that race permeates our societal structures and schools and churches.

I attended a funeral recently and noticed that the only people of color in the room were the Navy officers performing the military rites. I wondered how common this situation was for the officers. Later that same day, when I drove past Plantation Drive, I hoped those military officers didn't have to pass that same street on their way out of town.

People who don't live in the American South can't imagine how often, in our daily lives, we have to step around artifacts of slavery. People get married at plantation venues. College students pass Civil War monuments on their way to class. Confederate flags are still displayed on license plates and outside restaurants and homes.

And it isn't just Civil War history that haunts us. The civil rights movement is still pretty fresh, historically and culturally.

In our local public schools, the civil rights movement is taught before slavery. Maybe because it's developmentally appropriate. Maybe because Martin Luther King Jr. Day is celebrated even in kindergarten. Maybe because it's easier to start with a "win."

Whatever the reason may be, starting with the civil rights movement is a little confusing for kids. They can tell a piece is missing. Why did Black people not have rights from the beginning? What did they need to be freed from in the first place?

I knew in my gut that we needed to tell the twins about slavery before they heard about it at school, especially because they were often the only Black kids in their classes. I just didn't have a road map for how to tell them. These are messy but necessary conversations.

I remembered a colleague telling me that Jewish families have to intentionally tell their children about the Holocaust. So before we talked to the twins, I asked several Jewish people how they'd learned about the Holocaust. (I'm a lot of fun at parties.) In Jewish families, sometimes the discussion is linked to Passover. Sometimes, it's handled by elders.

I also asked several Black friends how they'd learned about slavery. Some had learned from elders in their family. Others, though, had learned from being called an ugly name or—most remarkable to me—from attending a family reunion and trying to figure out why white people were there too.

Over the course of a few years, Bryan and I talked to the twins about slavery. Then we talked about civil rights.

I thought we'd done a decent job of prepping them so they wouldn't learn any of these historical truths without warning, alone, in school. But of course, no parent can anticipate all the ways the world can break your child's heart.

I thought I was educated about the civil rights struggle, but I'd never heard of the Birmingham Children's Crusade. I didn't know that in the spring of 1963, Black children peacefully marched from the Sixteenth Street Baptist Church to talk to the mayor about segregation, only to have police dogs and high-pressure fire hoses turned on them. I didn't know that at least six hundred children were reportedly arrested and put on school buses and taken to jail.

I've lived in the South my whole life and had never studied this event, so KD had to learn about it, alone, at her new school. And then she started having nightmares.

Of course she did. The kids in those pictures looked like her.

Several years earlier, I had to leave the room when KD's sweet little six-year-old voice said, "I can sit anywhere I want to on the bus now because of Rosa Parks." She sounded so hopeful. She didn't yet know that Rosa Parks wasn't the end of the story—but I did. I didn't want her to see my tears.

These weren't just history lessons for our family anymore. This was now personal for me.

Of course, it should have been personal for me all along; it's always been personal for people of color. Before we adopted the twins, I'd had the privilege of distance.

So here's what I say to white people considering adopting, especially transracially, after these very violent, past few years: *Only adopt if your heart can handle seeing videos and images of children and young adults who look like your children being shot. You will be overwhelmed by these images. You will be changed by them. You will take every one of these incidents personally.*

I met a Methodist pastor from New Orleans once who told me a story about his neighborhood during Hurricane Katrina. It's actually a well-documented incident.

As a mom of Black children, I hoped I'd misunderstood it. As a white person, though, I kind of knew in my bones that it was true.

After Hurricane Katrina, a large group of people were stranded in the American Can Apartments, a mixed-income, mixed-race condominium complex in Mid-City. Of those stranded in the building, 170 were residents and 75 were people from the neighborhood. Many were elderly or handicapped.

For days, helicopters flew over New Orleans on search and rescue missions. John Keller, an ex-Marine, used fire extinguisher powder to paint a message on the roof that they needed food and water, and some Black residents stood on the roof and waved at the helicopters. The helicopters hovered but wouldn't land.

Then John Keller, himself a Black man, had the idea to take all the Black people off the roof and put white people on the roof instead. This included white people in wheelchairs.

Within fifteen minutes, the helicopter landed. And soon, food and water were falling from the sky.

I'm not saying the helicopter pilot was racist. I'm sure the pilot wasn't even aware of the bias. But it was there. I'm also not saying that New Orleans has a bigger race problem than the rest of us. This bias is everywhere.

What I am saying is that this story unflinchingly illustrates our racial prejudices as a society. This story is about how people with white skin are seen as more valuable or more deserving than people with brown skin.

I can't change the racial dynamics in my town or state or country. But I can get up on the roof and wave my arms around as if my life depended on it. In reality, my twins' lives kind of do depend on it—which means my life, as their mom, depends on it too.

My twins will be driving soon. Within a year, I won't be there at traffic stops to make sure they keep their hands where the police can see them at all times. I won't be there if the police assume KD is a young Black man because she has short hair and wears boys' athletic clothing. I won't be there if someone decides the twins look suspicious driving up to our house.

Having white parents won't mean anything when they are on their own.

We recently moved from the country into town. We love being in downtown Athens, and we love that the twins are now at a diverse high school. We wanted to move, in part, so they wouldn't feel like the only Black kids in their classes or on their sports teams.

I didn't anticipate, though, the economic differences of our new neighborhood. It took a comment from Elizabeth to draw my attention to it.

"I'm glad there are more people in our neighborhood now that look like me," she said shortly after we moved. "But I think most of them are homeless."

It was a real gut punch.

We live in a neighborhood that's pretty common in smaller Southern cities. It's blended racially but not economically. It has a homeless shelter and public housing but also lovely homes. It's diverse but still divided.

Living here is definitely better for our family than living near those cotton fields, but raising these beautiful Black girls of ours is still complicated. It's messy and beautiful and impossible and grace filled.

We're still in the thick of it. We aren't done being changed by our twins.

So I'll keep asking for help. I'll keep making mistakes. I'll keep waving my arms around on the rooftops. I'll keep seeing life through this new lens. I'll keep learning.

How has being a mom changed the way you view the world? What new lenses have you been given?

Is there a time when your worldview was rocked by something your kids discovered?

CHAPTER 17

Start practicing the art and etiquette of glomming.

GLOM ON TO: to become attached or stuck to something

It's important to know one's gifts. I've recently decided that I'm gifted at glomming on to other people. It's how I've survived.

This ability to glom on to others has taken many forms over the course of my life, but it usually starts with me walking into a room and confessing that I don't know what I'm doing and that I need help. I hope my vibe is less "damsel in distress" and more "Amelia Bedelia meets Jack Black."

I've glommed as a young clergywoman, a panicked mom, a new writer, a Gen Xer who struggles with technology, and a disoriented tourist.

Recently, I flew to Frankfurt, Germany, en route to Florence, Italy. I'm not a super-savvy traveler, so I knew it would be a bit tricky to make the connection. It was the first time I'd flown to Europe alone, and I don't know German. I also hadn't slept much on the plane.

When we landed, I followed most of the passengers from my plane to a customs line, only to draw exasperated pointing from the officials. Apparently, that wasn't the line I needed to be in, though I'm still not sure why. So I raced across the airport to the correct line, which wasn't moving fast at all.

"This always happens to me in Frankfurt," a woman next to me said.

This was a person who'd been to Frankfurt before and was thus my new best friend! I asked where she was going, and she said Florence (same! same! same!), but she wasn't hopeful she'd make the connection. I asked if I could please follow her once we got through customs.

And man, did I stay on her heels. We ran down long corridors, carried our bags up flights of stairs, and raced for a connecting bus. Someone yelled at us in German. They sounded angry. But everything sounds angry in German, so maybe they were just saying, "Y'all are fast! Way to go!"

When we finally found the elevator down to the bus, we heard our names being announced over the PA system. We jumped on the bus at the last second, sweaty and triumphant.

I thanked the woman profusely. I never saw her again, on purpose. I didn't ask for her help once we got to Florence. I sensed I'd used up all my goodwill with her.

Part of the art of glomming is that you can't push it. There's a fine line between glomming and mooching. I never want to overask for help.

The older I get, the more and more impressed I am with people who are truly generous—with information, talents, joy, and kindness. I adore people who are quick with "Me too!" and "Here's what I've learned." There's a bigheartedness in certain people that makes them glow.

I have a friend who laughs easily and loudly and often. He's genuine in his easy-to-tickle-ness, so he makes people around him feel much funnier than they actually are. It's delightful. Sure, he could withhold his laughter, but why? It's a renewable resource.

I practice this same enthusiasm with standing ovations and praising anyone who does anything brave. Because why not? It doesn't cost me anything. I don't want to be stingy with my cheering.

I have to believe that generosity comes back around. It's a lot like glomming. If you want to be blessed by it, you need to extend it. What I'm saying is this: don't just glom on to others—allow them to glom on to you. We all know a little more about something than someone else, and so we can all help that someone else navigate it.

I'm your girl if you need help in the Detroit airport. I can also help with potty training, college applications in the fine arts world, recipes for appetizers, IEP meetings, where to eat in Athens, what not to do with Black hair, how to feed big groups of teenagers, and how to grow flowers in the South. I'm not an expert in any of these areas, but I've learned enough to share what I know.

But I can't help you (or myself) with the

Frankfurt airport. I couldn't get through that place again if my life depended on it.

Have you ever been in a "Frankfurt" situation, where you needed to glom on to someone to help you navigate?

What are some areas, gifts, or experiences you can share with someone who needs help?

CHAPTER 18

Start holding up mirrors.

I'VE STARTED A list of things I wish we'd known when we adopted the twins. This isn't to beat myself up; it's to help someone who finds themselves in a similar situation with a transracial adoption. I've made notes about the best hair and skin products. I've written down suggestions about how to behave in a Black beauty shop. I've learned the hard way that visitors to a Black church should eat a big breakfast and always bring a Bible.

There's one area, though, that's hard for me to write about without feeling shame. It has to do with mirrors. As in community mirrors. All children need people who look like them to help guide and teach them. We did a lot of things right with the twins in those first years, but one area where we fell short was in not surrounding them with people of color who could inspire them.

I began to sense this when the twins were toddlers and we visited my mother at the high school where she worked. When I handed KD to my mom's friend, who was Black, KD started crying. She stopped, though, when another teacher, who was white, took her. The same thing happened with Elizabeth. It was weird and very embarrassing.

Then the same pattern played out again in another social situation. The twins cried whenever a Black woman held them. I was mortified.

I eventually faced the hard truth that the only Black women the twins had been around were either combing out their hair at the beauty shop or giving them shots at the pediatrician's office. Unintentionally, I had set up a dynamic that had caused the twins to associate Black women with physical discomfort.

From that point on, I became more intentional about bringing people of color into their lives. I thought we were making some progress, but then I found another area we'd neglected.

A few years ago, I signed my family up to attend a Presbyterian conference about racism. I was really excited to tell the twins that everyone speaking and preaching that weekend was Black.

As we were walking home from the first session, KD said something about the worship leaders being really dressed up. At first, I was a bit confused that she'd point this out. The worship leaders in our denomination almost always dress up. This is all the twins have really seen at church.

But then it hit me: what the twins hadn't seen was Black men and women dressed up *because they were in leadership positions*. Almost all the adults—especially leaders—in their lives were white. There were Black employees at their elementary school, but they weren't teachers or administrators.

As an ordained clergywoman, I know that what children see matters. I know that it's important for girls to see women in leadership positions—in science and medicine, in law and engineering. And I especially know that having role models of your same race are important. I love the quote from Marian Wright Edelman that says, "You can't be what you can't see."

And yet I was unprepared for the impact the movie *Hidden Figures* had on Elizabeth when I took her to see it in second grade. We were both inspired by these women, and we talked on the way home about how glad we were that someone had made this movie so that we could learn about them.

Once we were home, I started dinner and laundry. After a bit, I realized I hadn't seen Elizabeth for a while, so I went looking for her. She was in her room, with her paper and pencils out on her desk. She'd pulled her toy cash register out of the closet and was using it as an adding machine. She was working really hard on her math, telling me that she was practicing what they did in the movie.

Elizabeth embraced the example of the *Hidden Figures* heroines with an enthusiasm that was personal and urgent. I hadn't expected the movie to create such a clear cause and effect relationship. It was like she'd been unbelievably thirsty, and these women had appeared as a cool drink of water. As her mother, even I didn't know she'd been that thirsty.

Bryan and I love these girls to the moon and back. We can read and study and listen until the end of time, but we will never know what it's like to walk in the world as Black women.

But you know who does? Black women.

The first time Elizabeth went to the beauty shop to get long braids, she got quite a few "Yes, Queen!" and "Look at you, girl!" declarations. These beautiful Black women knew, from experience, that this daughter of mine needed to be built up before being sent out into the world. They were gassing her up. I've noticed that parents of Black children often work hard to instill this sense of confidence and worthiness in their own children and in all children.

The twins need people outside our white family to tell them that they are beloved and cherished. The world will try to tell them in a hundred different ways who they are and who they aren't allowed to be, but if they know their intrinsic worth, those destructive voices can't do as much harm.

When the twins were in elementary school, we often visited a Black Presbyterian church several towns away. One Sunday after service, we tried to load all four kids back into our minivan, but everyone was grumpy and hungry. I found myself questioning whether our visits to this church were even appropriate.

As we were about to leave, an older woman, a true deaconess with a flowery hat, slowly made her way over to our car. Leaning through the front window, she said, "Thank you for raising our girls."

I was speechless.

There was a long silence on the ride home. Finally, I turned to Bryan.

"Did she say 'our girls,' or did I mishear her?"

She'd definitely said "our."

There were a thousand reasons for that woman to have not wished us well—a white family she'd never met. Yet she'd extended her generosity and grace. More importantly, she'd claimed and blessed the twins.

When the twins entered their new high school, I expected that someone would call at least one of them an "Oreo"—and they did. Our twins are African American girls being raised in a white family, so they often feel caught between two worlds. So, the Oreo comment wasn't especially creative or hurtful.

But some of the other comments—and the unspoken meaning behind them—really surprised me.

For back-to-school shopping, KD had asked for Air Jordans—preferably the Air Jordan 1 Retro High OG in "University Blue," which cost over $300. I thought that was ridiculously expensive for shoes, so I'd ordered some knock-off Jordans from Amazon for $40.

Shoes are shoes, right? Are legit Jordans really that different than FZUU High-Top Leather Street Sneakers? We aren't a name-brand kind of family, I reasoned.

But she came home from the first week of school complaining about her blue and white FZUU sneakers. By the second week, she refused to wear them and instead wore her old running shoes to school.

Finally, I asked what the big deal was about her shoes and why she was being so difficult.

"People keep asking me if I have these cheap shoes because my parents are white."

Oh.

"Did you tell them that it isn't because we're white but because we are frugal?" I asked.

She stared at me blankly. Before she left the room, she muttered, "My friends who live in public housing have real Jordans."

Well, OK, then.

Clearly, this wasn't just about shoes.

Whenever a parenting issue blindsides me, I start asking around for guidance. In this case, even my white-mom friends were like, "Anna, shoes matter. You know this."

I guess I did know that, culturally, shoes do matter. But since I, personally, don't care about expensive shoes, I didn't think my kids would.

But my kids aren't middle-aged white ladies. They're Black teen girls being raised by white people while attending a predominantly Black high school.

It's a lot to navigate.

Before I'd even finished asking one of my Black friends about the shoe situation, she stopped me and said, "Get KD the damn shoes."

Even though I didn't think it made much sense, I ordered KD the Air Jordans. When she wore them to school, a kid said, "You're Black now!"

There is so much to unpack in that sentence that I don't even know where to begin. But I do know this: Me declaring that shoes shouldn't matter doesn't make them not matter to this particular kid of mine.

I know that some people will read this and think, "Families in public housing shouldn't waste their money on expensive shoes," or, "Maybe your family should take a stand and not give into peer pressure." Both of those might be true. But this also might be the thinking of someone who already has a fair amount of status.

I don't need expensive shoes for someone to think I'm well-off. I'm pretty sure my straight teeth and dyed hair and yoga clothes do that work for me. I don't think of myself as wealthy, but I'm writing these words from a nice house in the middle of a workday. I don't care what kind of shoes I wear because I have the luxury of not caring.

The shoe situation reminds me a lot of the steep learning curve I had with the twins' hair. Not only learning how to do their hair but more so understanding why it mattered so much. With our first two kids, I never thought about their hair, except when they needed a haircut.

The twins were still infants when a Black man told me I needed to do something about their hair because they looked like boys. I finally caught on that people, especially Black people, would know that the twins were being well taken care of by their hair.

Even if that didn't make a lot of sense to me, I found a beauty shop and made sure their hair looked presentable. Especially when it was time to send pictures to their birth mother, their hair needed to look great. It was one way of showing her that the twins were in good hands.

There are plenty of days when I worry that we're botching this transracial adoption thing, including the days when the color of my skin makes my kids' days harder. Maybe I bought KD those shoes as a kind of reparation. Maybe it was motivated by white guilt. Maybe I just decided it was a battle I didn't need to fight.

Most likely, I bought her the shoes because I finally realized it was a small thing I could do to help her feel more confident at her new school. I don't have to fully understand it to believe KD when she says it matters.

It's not just the twins who need mirrors—people who can inspire them and reflect back to them their intrinsic goodness and worth. *I* also need mirrors. That is, I need people in the Black community to hold up a mirror so I can see myself clearly.

Even if that means changing my opinion and buying my kid "the damn shoes."

Have you ever been surprised by something or someone that inspired your kid or provided a mirror for them?

Could you perhaps need someone to hold a mirror up to you? Is there a situation in your life right now that you could stand to reevaluate? What's your equivalent of buying "the damn shoes"?

CHAPTER 19

Start building something new.

WHEN BRYAN GOT back from driving our son to college in Michigan, I was somehow shocked that Caleb wasn't in the car with him. I was a mess. Before Bryan's legs were even out of the car, I announced that we were going to need to move because our house, without the big kids, was making me sad.

While Bryan acknowledged that it was indeed the end of an era, he wasn't as distraught as me. "We'll just have to build something new" was his wise, gut-wrenching, and hope-filled plan.

Even with Bryan's advice, I didn't handle the transition well. I was stuck emotionally. I could only

145

see things that were broken. Some of my kids were having a hard time, the election was looming, and life felt heavy.

I knew I had so much to be thankful for, but I struggled to access that part of my heart. I was getting on my own nerves.

So I sent out a Bat-Signal. I asked people I knew personally and online for ideas about how to develop more gratitude in my life. I needed some practical ways to shift my focus.

People had great suggestions, including apps and elaborate journaling. But in the end, I landed on a very simple practice: Every night, I would write down five things I was thankful for that day.

For the past four years, this practice has seen me through our ordinary days and our big changes. I'm now on my seventh notebook. It's really helpful to look back through them—even to look back on the days when I was clearly digging deep for new material. (I was thankful one day in April 2021 to not be the queen of England . . . ? I'd either just started watching *The Crown* or thought I couldn't handle any new duties.)

This nightly ritual feels like prayer and journaling and sleuthing all at the same time. Mostly, it's a good reminder of the ridiculous abundance of love and goodness in my life.

I tend to catastrophize and regularly declare that we "gave it our best shot yet all hope is lost." Now, I have over seven thousand documented observations, specific to me, that argue otherwise. Reassurances written in your own handwriting are hard to dismiss.

The biggest benefit of this practice, though, is the way it has shifted how I walk through my days. I actually look for things I can add to my notebook.

If one of my kids has strep throat, I decide to be thankful for access to good medical care and inexpensive antibiotics. If I miss my big kids, I remember to be thankful that they love their colleges. If I'm tired and need a break, I remember that I'm truly thankful for coffee and that school is open post-COVID.

Often, my list includes simple pleasures, such as fresh grapefruit, as well as holy gifts such as adoption. I love that these big and small things are all mixed up in my notebooks.

Just like they're mixed up in my messy, ordinary, yet amazing life.

But it isn't enough to just be thankful for thankfulness's sake. Gratitude should be fuel for our actions. It should especially be fuel for building something new.

I'm in the process of figuring out our next era. What's next for us as a family? What's next for me as a mom? What's next for me as Anna?

My hunch is that advocacy and activism are gaining momentum in both my heart and mind. Black Lives Matter protests and Pride parades are now part of our family's life together. All of it is a way of acknowledging how much work there is to do—and how much I've been changed by my children.

I hope I'd still be out in the streets if I didn't have gay or Black kids. But I *do* have gay and Black kids, and that's motivation enough to use what little influence I have for inclusion and social justice.

I'm sensing that advocacy is part of my calling. It's hard to know where to start, but there's a photo of a woman climbing a flagpole that has served as a North Star for me.

On June 27, 2015, an African American woman named Bree Newsome scaled the flagpole at the

South Carolina State House to bring down the Confederate flag. Ten days earlier, Dylann Roof had killed nine church members at Emmanuel African Methodist Episcopal Church in Charleston, South Carolina. It had been a racially motivated mass shooting.

Following the massacre, there was a public push to take down the Confederate flag. Bree and other activists thought it was taking too long, so she took the matter into her own hands.

The images from that day show such fierce bravery and such determination for justice that they make me teary. At the same time, I feel so convicted by Bree's actions that I want to look away.

A few years ago, I helped with a forum on dialogue about race. The keynote speaker, Dr. Bettina Love, mentioned Bree's heroism. In addition to being inspired all over again by Bree, I also learned something important about being more than just an ally to the oppressed.

In the videos and pictures from that historic day, you can see a man in a construction hat at the bottom of the pole. I'd assumed he worked on the grounds. But actually, he was a white environmental activist from North Carolina named James Tyson.

In several news articles, he was listed as her "spotter," but he was so much more than that.

In addition to teaching Bree to climb, he helped her into the fenced area and stayed at the bottom of the pole while she climbed. He was arrested with her, but he didn't appear on talk shows with her. He stayed in the background.

The most amazing fact about James Tyson was that he put his hand on the flagpole.

At one point, the police threatened to tase the metal pole—to send electricity through it—if Bree didn't come down. In response, she yelled down at the police that her climbing was a nonviolent act.

At the bottom of the pole, James implored the police not to harm her. As the situation escalated, James put his hand on the flagpole. His simple action meant that if she were electrocuted, then he would be too.

The same people who'd been willing to tase a pole with a Black woman climbing it would not tase a pole with a white person touching it.

This action cost James very little. He knew that as a white man, he had influence and clout. He used his white male privilege to protect someone who needed it.

Bree was quoted as saying, "He refused to let go until I was back on the ground."

This image of placing one's hand on the flagpole has stayed with me. I keep thinking about ways that I've missed the opportunity to do this for people of color, for LGBTQIA+ people, for Muslims, and for immigrants.

At the race forum, Dr. Love stated that people of color don't need any more allies; what they need are co-conspirators.

In *I'm Still Here: Black Dignity in a World Made for Whiteness*, author Austin Channing Brown writes about white people coming up to her after she speaks at conferences. These people confess to her their own racism or the times they've been complicit in racist actions.

They don't do this with her white colleagues, she notes. She's decided that these people want absolution from her—but that this is too much for her to carry. "I am not a priest for the white soul," she writes.

Instead, she asks them, "What are you going to do differently?"

It's a great question.

Here's what I'm ready to do differently: I'm going to put my hand on the flagpole. It's that simple and that hard.

It's what building something new will look like for me.

What's next for you? What do you want to do differently?

Also, you are doing great! Keep going!

Acknowledgments

THANKS FIRST AND foremost to my husband, Bryan, who is kind, loyal, tenacious, loving, and unfailingly optimistic. Thank you for being my best friend and patient partner for the past three decades. I don't deserve you, but I'm so glad you're mine.

My amazing kids—Caroline, Caleb, KD, and Elizabeth—remind me daily of God's goodness. Being your mom is the greatest gift of my life. Thank you for letting me write about our life together.

Thank you to all the wonderful people who believed I could write a book and who encouraged me to see it through, especially my chosen sisters for life, Mary Barnett, Deborah Googe, and Susan Atchley; my spiritual director and friend Karen Kassinger; my earliest blog readers, including my mom's friends and the members of Oconee Presbyterian Church; Rev. Steve Price; Rev. Renee DuBose; Sally and Jim Richardson; Sara and John Cawley; Tricia Dillon-Thomas; Greg and Shannon Kershner; my aunt Linda; and Bob Googe.

I have amazing parents, who made sure I felt loved every single day of my life. My mom instilled in me a love of reading, and my dad was unwavering in his (sometimes delusional) belief in my abilities as a writer.

Big love and thanks to my brother Miles Thomas, who calms me down, and my brother Clay Thomas, who hypes me up.

I probably wouldn't have survived motherhood without the people who have helped me regain my footing and/or helped me not lose my ever-loving mind: the lady in the preschool parking lot who showed me that it's okay to not have everything under control, Rev. Pam Driesell, Tina Tinsley, Dr. Brett Atchley, Dr. Karl Barnett, Melynda McCutcheon, Rebecca Thomas, my nieces and nephews, yoga teachers and classmates who kindly avert their eyes when I cry through class, Josh and Kate Hawk, all the therapists in our lives, plus whoever invented Wellbutrin.

I was guided by the wonderful writing workshop leader Jen Louden and our fabulous group of women in Mexico, especially Beth Howard, who encouraged me to keep writing, even if the publishing world intimidated me. Also, I learned so much from writing retreat leaders Allison K. Williams and Dinty Moore and our group in Italy. You inspired, encouraged, and challenged me in the gentlest ways possible. Thanks also to Rebecca Morrison, who was incredibly generous with her knowledge of the essay publishing world.

I am grateful to my editor, Angela Wiechmann, who made this book so much clearer and fiercer. If there's an award for editors who are both efficient and kind, I'd like to nominate you. Thank you to the team at Beaver's Pond Press for taking a chance on me. I am especially thankful for Abbie Phelps, my project manager, who took us across the finish line with confidence and grace. Yawen Chien created the beautiful illustration on the front cover; her warm and joyful spirit shone through into her artwork and I love it so much. Thank you also to Alysson Bourque at Expound Publicity for her patience and expertise. Ruth Bullivant gave shape and clarity to the book, all the way from England.

I have such deep gratitude for our communities in Athens, Georgia, and Montreat, North Carolina, who have loved my children so well, including educators and advocates; Novella Edwards; tutors and therapists; a slew of very patient UGA students who have been our sitters for years; fine arts mentors and athletic coaches; youth directors and camp counselors; Catherine and Fletcher Wilson; Laura Cunningham and Scott Ramsey; John Richardson; Nancy Jones; Kate O'Reilly; and all those who have prayed for my sweet family over the years.

I am in awe of the ways God has guided and provided for me. It is only by God's grace that I have words to share. I'm so honored that you, lovely reader, chose to read my book. Thank you for coming on this journey with me.

About the Author

ANNA MCARTHUR is a mom to four kids, including two recent college graduates and twin girls who are high schoolers. She is a blogger, newspaper guest columnist, and contributor to parenting magazines and websites, including Her View from Home and the Motherly Collective. Anna's essays have recently been published by *Grown and Flown* and *Business Insider*.

A graduate of Clemson University and Columbia Theological Seminary, Anna lives in Athens, Georgia, with her husband, Bryan, and their teen-aged girls, who are much cooler than her. Anna loves to read, garden, hike, and eat dips for dinner.

This is her first book.